Foreword by Dr. Khadijia White-Thomas
Featuring, Chucks And Pearls And Black Girl Magic

A Book Of Poetry And Haikus By Robert L. Horton,
Author Of Released, Miscellaneous Pieces, And Fame.

Foreword

Amazing and Soul Touching!

As you read this book of poetry get ready to be blessed, inspired, and touched. Each poem will embrace you and express itself in awesome, unbounding love ~ soul touching. Robert and I share a mutual respect for life and the mindset to follow your passion and live your life's dream.

Throughout *Imagine,* Robert Horton brings forth faith-filled lines, verses, statements, and words brought to life in such a way that readers are enlightened through nuggets of wisdom, and fascinated by a style that touches the heart, mind, and soul.

Robert is a choice vessel to share brilliant poetry and *Imagine* captures the essence of that abundance which he reveals in this fascinating book. Whether you have been a devoted poetry lover, recently began reading poetry, or you are somewhere in between, *Imagine* will capture your heart and impact your vision of the world around you. Get ready to embark on the newness of nourishing your faith, creating transformation, and developing fresher perspectives through the *Imagine* journey.

Do you mind if I take a moment and share a few favorites? This is not an all-encompassing list. If I were to list each one, it would be the entire book! That being the case, the poetry I highlight below stands out to me and is worthy of special mention.

- *Imagine and Mental Therapy* are powerful and visionary.
- *Mentors, Keep Going, and For Your Consideration* deliver sound advice.
- *Chucks and Pearls and Black Girl Magic, Just Me,* and *Purposeful Living* illustrate confidence in womanhood.
- *The Art of Creating* and *Finish Strong* encourage remaining steadfast in your passion.
- *Can You* and *A Fulfilled Life* are just simply compelling.
- 9 *Beatitudes* and *The Lord Knows* purport treasures of elegance.
- *Borrowed Time, Signs for His Return,* and *Time* convey the philosophy of life.
- *The Pursuit, What People Need, Freedom or Defeat,* and *My Word* are captivating and to the point!
- *The Mind, Body, and Life* is the great depiction of the powerful three.

After reading *Imagine*, I encourage you to share it with others for amazement and for soul touching words. *Imagine* is brilliant and Robert, aka the Moody Poet, has continued to change the world with uplifting poetry.

Thank you, my friend, for sharing your extraordinary talent!

Dr. Khadijia White-Thomas, CEO/Founder Education Consultant/Business Strategist Decree Consulting and Publishing, LLC

Dedication

To Aunt Renee.
Thank you for your encouraging words. They lifted
me and made this book possible.

Table of Contents

Imagine if you believed you could.

Introduction Poem

<u>Borrowed Time</u>

God is the giver of life-
But it's borrowed time.
Grace is needed to live free of strife-
Peace is a treasure to find.

"What's borrowed, must be returned."

Imagine

Imagine joy and no sorrow,
Imagine the love that we shared today, reflected tomorrow.
Imagine peace and no hate,
Imagine if Heaven was everyone's fate.
Imagine no guns and no crime,
Imagine no sun because everyone shined.
Imagine no greed and no war,
Imagine no need to beg because no one was poor.
Imagine clean air and good health,
Imagine I am my brother's keeper as the new wealth.
Imagine no storms or natural disasters,
Imagine The Lord's return coming much faster.
Imagine no wickedness in high places,
Imagine mutual respect between all of the races.
Imagine walking in purpose,
Imagine The Golden Rule as your reasonable service.
Imagine reaching your destiny,
Imagine becoming all that you desire to be.

"Imagine with me."

A Nation In Peril

Let us cry out together,
Maybe collective prayer will make things better.
Or maybe we should write God a letter,
To turn from His wrath and displeasure.

So much division and war,
Natural disasters occur like never before.
Dead fish are washing upon the shore,
Proof that our planet can't take much more.

Each day brings more bloodshed,
Poor people struggle to get ahead.
With misinformation we are constantly fed,
So we focus on our differences instead.

These current conditions brought the flood,
Let's come together and walk-in love.
And create a world God is proud of,
That reflects His kingdom up above.

**"We must learn to live together as brothers
or perish together as fools."
-Dr. King**

The Mind, Body, And Life

The mind and body go through a lot,
It's not easy being here-
This life takes all that you got,
Especially when the path is not clear.

How do you know which way to go,
How do you know what's best to do-
When should you go fast or take it slow,
When should you stop or see it through.

Work is taxing on the body,
Stress wreaks havoc on the mind-
Like a boat tossed in a tsunami,
And inner strength is hard to find.

Is life a curse or a blessing,
What is all this suffering about-
Many of life's unanswered questions,
Lead to more worry and doubt.

Is there really a promised land,
If so, when will we get there-
By and by, will we really understand,
Or will the wheat be eaten by the tares.

Life is a perilous quest,
And the journey is long-
The mind and body need plenty of rest,
For both to carry on.

"The struggle is real."

Full Circle (The Redemption Of A 15 yr. Old Run Away)

For freedom I could not wait,
But it was a costly mistake.
I left and didn't care,
I really thought I was going somewhere.
But as I traveled,
The road began to unravel.
I was afraid and lost,
I didn't count up the cost.
I was mad, young, and dumb,
And to immature whims, I succumbed.
I was broken and without hope,
The wilderness had become unbearable to cope.
I turned to go back,
But didn't know where I was at.
Suddenly, I realized,
That before destruction, there is pride.
The pain inside would not subside,
Then I fell on my knees and cried.
Running away was a bad choice,
Then out of nowhere I heard a soft voice.
It said, "**Return Unto Me,**
I will save your soul and set you free."
I apologized for what I had done,
And received His grace like the prodigal son.
Then the road back home became clear,
And never again will I veer.

"My prodigal son experience."

Positivity (Note To Myself)
For Dr. Sheka Houston

Don't ever give up,
Give yourself another day-
Your wheels aren't permanently stuck,
Soon you'll be on your way.

Don't count yourself out,
Be a hopeful referee-
You deserve the benefit of the doubt,
Soon you'll reach your destiny.

Stay in the game,
Fight a little longer-
Sunshine comes after the rain,
Failure is how muscles grow stronger.

Always believe in yourself,
Like you encourage others to do-
Inner peace is true wealth,
Start showing love to you.

"Have you had your plus sign today."
-Prince

Depression

My joy is gone,
It's hard to pretend-
The tunnel is long,
And no light at the end.

Staring out my window,
New day, but same song-
With no place to go,
Everything that could, went wrong.

I feel out of place,
No strength to carry on-
My life is a waste,
Down here I don't belong.

No appetite for food,
It's a struggle to bathe-
Always in a sad mood,
Negative thoughts keep me enslaved.

My house is a mess,
I rarely get out of bed-
Suicidal from being depressed,
I'm better off dead.

"The sunken place."

Death
(The Grin Remover)

What removes a grin,
Good times never last-
When loved ones pass,
That's when sadness begins.

One minute you're up,
The next moment you're down-
Happiness can't be found,
And life doesn't mean as much.

Life is but a tease,
Death is a formidable foe-
It follows like a shadow,
Constantly under siege.

My grin is gone forever,
This pain won't subside-
So many tears I've cried,
Nothing can make it better.

"Death is hard to process when life with someone is all you know."

Signs For His Return

We live,
But cannot get along-
Respect for elders is gone,
We have no more love to give
Where did we go wrong.

We age,
But do not grow spiritually older-
Hearts have become colder,
We are easily enraged-
Criminals get bolder.

We die,
Promising lives are cut short-
Some choose to abort,
We live a lie-
We must answer to a higher court.

God is good,
But His grace won't last forever-
We need to get our lives together,
We do not do as we should-
Unhealthy ties we need to sever.

The next life awaits,
Jesus is coming back soon-
Blood will cover the moon,
Repent before it's too late-
Prepare for The Bridegroom.

"Behold I come quickly."
Revelation 22:12

The End Times

An army of bad men are coming,
And without provocation they will start gunning.

Countless souls will meet their fate,
Grief will be unleashed from the carnage of hate.

Violence will increase from the wrath of the
beast,
Death and destruction from the absence of peace.

Lawlessness is the new order of the land,
Who in that day will be able to stand.

**"For then there will be great distress,
unequaled from the beginning of the world
until now, and never to be equaled again."
Matthew 24:21**

Forsaken

How did I get here,
And when can I leave-
The path is not clear,
Betrayal I could never conceive.

What good is a sign,
If you cannot see-
Blindly existing marking time,
And no one to rescue me.

My purpose I never found,
Could not overcome my raw deal-
The only peace is underground,
What does not kill you, eventually will.

Life just threw me away,
Forsaken by family and friends-
Dying alone is a slow decay,
The pain remains until the end.

**"You never know where life might find you.
Especially when you can't find yourself."**

The Blessed Ones

Blessed are the unborn,
Those who did not make it here-
No heart to be filled with scorn,
No eyes to be filled with tears.

No hurtful words to hear,
No evil acts to see-
No shame or living in fear,
No uncertain destiny.

No guilt or living with pain,
No sins to confess-
No scars or incessant rain,
No friends who could care less.

No wishing you were somewhere else,
No insecurities to hide-
No thoughts of harming yourself,
No mourning those who died.

"It takes so much to live. There is so much
that you have to deal with on earth.
Sometimes I wonder if life is worth living."

The Human Condition

When you have more than you need,
When more than enough is stored up-
Too much is never enough,
Excess is a function of greed.

With so many in lack,
Others need what you can spare-
Open up your heart and share,
What you give always comes back.

War is everywhere,
What caused our human condition-
Why is there so much hatred and division,
Not enough people who care.

Life is a difficult maze,
But can be amazing-
Joy is what giving brings,
Then we will see better days.

"Give, and it will be given back to you."
Luke 6:38

When A Seed Dies

When a seed dies,
It cries on the inside.

Turmoil-
In the belly of the soil.

As it brings forth life,
The seed dies twice.

**"Unless a kernel of wheat falls to the
ground and dies, it remains only a single
seed. But if it dies, it produces many
seeds."
John 12:24**

The Art Of Grafting
(For Neeka Grafton, A Gifted Soul Child)

I'm giving the best of me,
To be grafted into you-
This is my calling to do,
So you can be set free.

I cast poetic lines,
Throughout this book-
Hoping to set my hook,
Inside your heart and mind.

We must self-reflect to discover,
Fear and doubt are cast aside-
A soul child with nothing to hide,
Truth builds trust within each other.

Live your life to inspire,
Your light is for someone's night-
Pursue dreams and keep hope in sight,
Being selfless is a noble desire.

**"It's time to create that.
What you put out, will manifest back."**

Poetry And Me

Sometimes it is rife with strife.
Like, when I get stuck, and wanna give up.

Other times it's smooth, and I find my groove.
When the pen is my friend, it seems there is no
end.

But those who write, pay a tremendous price.
Like burning the midnight oil, and many sleepless
nights.

You put your work on hold and try to walk away.
But the burden becomes more bold, and never
goes away.

Poetry aint always nice.
It requires Godly patience, and personal sacrifice.

**"The words you read
were not easily conceived."**

Instant Gratification

Young minds have no concept of time.
They want it now without delay-
But life does not work that way.

We live in a world that is fast paced,
And everything is a rat race.

Everyone wants to win-
But some struggle to jump in.

Life is like double dutch.
Let us build and lift each other up-
Words of encouragement mean so much.

**"Nothing comes overnight. Everyone has their
own pace to get there.
Begin your journey and it will inspire others
to do the same."**

A Cautionary Tale
(For My Dear, My Daughter Amaiya)

Deceit taste sweet,
Truth is bitter-
Don't trust everyone you meet,
Fake gold will glitter.

Eyes are the window,
But deceivers are bold-
Cunning is all they know,
Existing without a soul.

They devour at will,
No respecter of persons-
On assignment to kill,
Always scheming and lurking.

Pray and move wisely,
Pressure from peers resist-
Few deserve your company,
To your goals commit.

"We are living in some strange times Dear.
Move with caution. Everybody who says they
are with you, aint really with you. Keep your
circle small and hold your own."

The Grind

The place to begin, is within.
The time it takes to grow, is slow.
If you wanna go farther, you gotta work harder.
You gotta grind, if you wanna shine.

"Success is for serious strivers only."

The Mask We Wear

Each soul has a story,
That longs to be told-
Not for fame or glory,
Not even to be sold.

The mask is our boss,
That we wear each day-
But the soul bears the cost,
When the mask goes away.

"What we don't want seen, we hide.
Or at least we try too."

The Wayward Son

He was not strong enough,
So he did not make the team-
The sport was just too rough,
Now it's on to a new dream.

Not the most handsome guy,
He could never get a date-
Never gave his alarm a try,
And was always running late.

He could not cook worth a lick,
Everything he made, he burned-
Hung out with the wrong clique,
Life lessons never learned.

In class he misbehaved,
He never liked to read-
He always made bad grades,
So his momma told him to leave.

He could not keep a job,
Got fired from each one-
Went around like a slob,
The life of a wayward son.

"Unfortunately, some never find their way."

9 Beatitudes
(For The 9 Parts Of The Soul)
For my niece, Kennedy C. Horton

Beatitude 1
You have purpose under the sun.

Beatitude 2
Cultivate the gifts that God has given to you.

Beatitude 3
You own the key to your destiny. You can become anything you desire to be.

Beatitude 4
God knocks at the door. New life begins when you invite Him in. Into your cup He will pour.

Beatitude 5
You must continue to strive. Realize there is purpose in your pain.
Even when victory is attained, more is required in order to maintain.

Beatitude 6
You must never quit. Keep going and continue growing.
The redeemed of The Lord shall outlast. Stay strong and be of good courage because this too shall pass.

Beatitude 7

The goal of your soul is to make it to Heaven. To get anywhere you must first prepare. Your life is precious to Him, so handle with care.

Beatitude 8

Straight is the gate and narrow is the way. Each soul will give an account for their deeds one day. So count up the cost and do not veer off. Earthly gains are in vain if your soul is lost.

Beatitude 9

Take advantage of your time. Do not waste what you cannot replace.
Answer the call and do not delay. You may not get another day.

"The words that I speak unto you, they are spirit, and they are life."
John 6:63

Mentors

Fill me, and I will pour.
Affirm me, and I will soar.
Polish me, and I will shine.
Guide me, and I won't roam blind.

"Effective leaders will affect future leaders."

Finish Strong

It doesn't matter where you start,
Even Christ was born in a manger-
What defiles, proceed from the heart,
Do not be reckless in your anger.

There will be obstacles along the way,
But you must overcome-
You will have what you say,
Power is within the tongue.

For this journey you will be equipped,
You will arrive at the appointed time-
Remind yourself, that you got this,
Bring others along as you climb.

The prize is worth the hardships,
What you went through, made you-
Life rewards those who do not quit,
Finish strong is what you must do.

"Finishing the race justifies being in it."

<u>Time</u> (The Universal Curse)

Time has one job,
And that is to pass-
Time moves fast,
Because it robs.

       Time does not heal,
       It only takes-
       Time never runs late,
       And cannot be killed.

Time is a cruel father,
And is always against you-
Time limits what you can do,
And is undefeated, so why bother.

       Time runs out,
       And cannot be replaced-
       Time is wasted in haste,
       Then missed like rain in a drought.

Time has no secrets,
It always tells-
Time will be cast into hell,
With death attached to it.

       Time was created first,
       And keeps you pressed-
       Time leaves you under duress,
       The universal curse.

"Once you are born, you are on the clock."

When Tragedy Strikes

Life can be so nice,
Prince told us this-
But when tragedy strikes,
Targets will not be missed.

When mother nature attacks,
It could be bad for you-
Some things you cannot get back,
And there is nothing you can do.

Your life turned upside down,
And your head hangs low-
In your tears you drown,
With no place to go.

Anyone can be touched,
No one is immune-
Precious moments mean so much,
But are gone to soon.

**"Lay not up for yourselves treasures upon earth,
where moth and rust doth corrupt and thieves
break in and steal."
Matthew 6:19**

Can You
(Being There For Others)

Can you spare to share,
Some of what you have-
And do you even care,
When someone else is sad.

Can you be a light,
When others cannot see-
Give hope in their darkest night-
Will your words set them free.

Can you lend an ear,
When someone needs to vent-
Are your intentions clear,
Is your time well spent.

Can you let people know,
How you really feel-
Do your actions show,
Do you always keep it real.

"Life is tough and it's getting tougher by the
minute. A lot of people are on edge.
A word of encouragement goes a long way. You
never know what people are going through."

Constructive Critique Or Hate Speech

I don't mind constructive critique,
Just speak the truth in love-
But I reject veiled hate speech,
Nothing you said was from above.

Many people rush to condemn,
But lack the courage to try-
Their outlook on life is grim,
And opportunities keep passing them by.

They believe it can be done better,
But never command the way-
The weak and strong should work together,
Striving to make a better day.

Words should be used to build,
Not to tear each other down-
Positive speech keeps everyone filled,
And lifts those who are on the ground.

**"If you are not building, you are tearing down.
There is no in-between."**

I'm Just Saying (For Your Consideration)

Work with what you got,
Sometimes a little means a lot.
Don't spend all your time on Tik Tok,
Pursue your dreams and never stop.

Some can't get out of bed,
Chronic pain makes them wish they were dead.
Some things are better left unsaid,
In order to lead you must be led.

Skies won't always be blue,
People will fail you.
You're a person too,
When others fall, be their rescue.

Everyone needs grace,
Give people their space.
Move at your own pace,
Life is a journey not a race.

"Consider your ways."
Haggai 1:5

The Beautiful Ones

They are sent by God to inspire,
To be a light, and take people higher-
The beautiful ones are greatly admired,
But they too have been through the fire.

Too many souls have been led astray,
Some beautiful ones have even lost their way-
Call out their names every time you pray,
No one is promised to see another day.

It rains on the just and the unjust,
Faith in The Most High is a must-
In Him alone place your hope and trust,
Why judge me when all return to dust.

We are only here for a little while,
All of us have our own personal trials-
Be the reason for someone else's smile,
Lend a hand and go that extra mile.

**"Everybody can be great
because everybody can serve."
-Dr. Martin Luther King Jr.**

Fruition

People sleep on the meek,
But they will inherit the earth.
Seeds sown will be reaped,
Know and value your worth.

"Let them doubt, you just keep the faith."

Behind The Scenes

I do not have it all together,
It just looks like I do–
My goal is to get better,
Behind the scenes, I am just like you.

Sometimes my self-esteem wanes,
My mood swings get me down–
Smiles help conceal unresolved pain,
Then I am no fun to be around.

It is easy to pretend,
Life is unfair and demanding-
It is rare to find a true friend,
Who will not judge but is understanding.

People need healed from past trauma,
Certain things take time to outgrow-
Without peace you only attract drama,
This is why so many plateau.

"Transparency."

Her Arrival
(The Return Of Daphne D. Hampton)

After many hours in the air,
She arrived home with God's care-
A surprise for her momma awaits,
Her baby is back in the United States.

Her momma is lovely as can be,
Apples rarely fall to far from the tree-
Tears of joy running down their face,
They receive each other with a warm embrace.

Her brother, daughter, and sons are overjoyed as
well,
Along with her grandkids, who she will have so
much to tell-
Precious moments like these are second to none,
The journey in happiness has now begun.

She is a Queen living out her dreams,
Those walking in purpose are on her team-
Every good thing she will possess,
And I am wishing you all the best.

"Welcome back home."

The Other Garden

The earth will be planted,
The biggest seed taken for granted.

In the other garden, sins will be pardoned,
And the hearts of men will not be hardened.

Jesus Christ will rule as King,
And God's love will reign supreme.

"Behold, I create new heavens and a new earth."
Isaiah 65:17

Life Is A Chess Game (Move Strategically)

Life is a chess game.
The worse move that you could make-
Is to remain the same.

Stay positive and do not complain.
Do not fall apart when it gets dark-
Be your own flame.

And do not be a side show.
Humble yourself and ask for help-
When you really don't know.

Think critically.
Do not blindly go with the flow-
Act independently.

Do not feed into what you used to do.
Plant new seeds-
And become a better you.

Life is a chess game.
Move strategically-
On others, never place the blame,
And take responsibility.

"Grow at your own pace but keep up."

Chucks And Pearls And Black Girl Magic
(The Rise Of The Incomparable Black
Woman) For Amanda Gorman

Chucks and Pearls for all the fine ladies and pretty
little girls,
Whose presence is felt all around the world.

You epitomize **Black Girl Magic**-
Dreams feed your self-esteem, and excellence is
your habit.

What the world needs, you possess-
Blessed, and highly favored, with a nation to
address.

Her time has come,
She is bold without fear-
Rose to the occasion like the sun,
And her message was clear.

It is time for her story,
Appointed for this day-
For America to reach its glory,
Black women will lead the way.

"God is within her; she will not fall."
Psalm 46:5

Confessions
(The Truth Revealed)

There is pain inside,
Outside is no better-
Salty tears will not subside,
Sullen, just like the weather.

Truth is hard to suppress,
Past time to speak out-
I found the courage to confess,
I struggle with fear and doubt.

Looks can be deceiving,
Smiles could be a mask-
Scriptures are for believing,
What is seen will not last.

God grant me the grace,
To have faith over fear-
To walk at your pace,
Please make my path clear.

**"Do not suppress what you are dealing with,
instead confess it.
And then begin your journey of healing and
walking by faith."**

Waning Youth

Where did my youth go,
Why did it leave-
Lord, please let me age slow,
Then die peacefully.

Body, mind, and soul,
In constant state of change-
In time we grow old,
Youth is hard to maintain.

**"Let their flesh be renewed like a child's.
Let them be restored as in the days of their
youth."
Job 33:25**

Nothing To Bargain With

In tears I put my chips down,
Then laid prostrate on the ground-
Men do not cry is a myth,
We have nothing to bargain with.

The lifted-up spirit will soon fall,
In shame they will lose it all-
The spirit of pride you must resist,
We have nothing to bargain with.

Proof of repentance is changed behavior,
The humble in spirit receive His favor-
Things we possess are given as gifts,
We have nothing to bargain with.

To redeem mankind Christ paid the cost,
And emptied His life upon the cross-
To the risen savior we must submit,
We have nothing to bargain with.

"For it is by grace you have been saved, through faith, and not of yourselves, it is a gift of God. Not by works, so that no man can boast."
Ephesians 2: 8-9

The War Between Spirit And Flesh

Be careful what you turn on,
You might struggle turning it off-
Some battles will never be won,
Some wins are just another loss.

Eyes want what they see,
Desires of the heart follow-
Some things you should let be,
Worldly pleasures will leave you hollow.

Temptation will lead you astray,
Some will never overcome-
Daily we need to pray,
 For God's will to be done.

Our spirit is in need,
It begs to be fed-
The flesh is easily deceived,
By God's voice we should

"The spirit gives life, the flesh counts for nothing."
John 6:63

Just Me

Just me is who I be,
I am more than what you heard and did not see.

Sometimes I am good,
And feel good about myself-
Sometimes I do not do as I should,
And wish that I was someone else.

It is not easy being me,
But I am striving to become the son that God wants
me to be.

Many judge from a lack of love and are quick to
condemn,
But we all need God's grace to navigate this world
of sin.

My eyes get weary,
My knees buckle sometimes-
But I know God is with me,
And the only friend of mine.

**"God is not through with me yet; I am still a work
in progress. I am striving to become the best
version of myself that I can be. I ask for your
prayers and patience."**

People
(Get Over Yourself)

What you do,
Others do too.

Some people think,
Their shit don't stink.

People are lame-
We are all the same.

**"None of us have any room to sit in judgment of
anyone else. All of us need a savior."**

A Fulfilled Life

On a quiet moonlit night,
I meditate and burn sage-
As I prepare to write,
Staring at a blank page.

Words on my heart to say,
I pray they will lift you-
And inspire hope along the way,
And your mind be made anew.

In life we get knocked down,
But giving up you must refrain-
Champions find a way to rebound,
To do it better and maintain.

May you find happiness in life,
May you discover your true self-
Your destiny comes with a price,
A fulfilled life is the new wealth.

"I pray that the words I write will inspire you to become the best version of yourself."

Little Chalk Lines
(Prayers For The City Of Chicago)

Stray bullets are blind,
Saddened by all the little chalk lines-
What God sees He pities,
Ugly times in a beautiful city.

Shameful when children are laid to rest,
Small bodies in caskets is hard to digest-
A depraved world where people are lost,
Countless tears bear the immeasurable cost.

Gone are the days of innocent play,
Now its duck quick from an incoming stray-
Today's youth are void of direction,
Rage run-amuck from lack of affection.

Life hurts when you are poor and black,
Traumatized youth have targets on their back-
Lord, we need you now like never before,
So little chalk lines won't be drawn anymore.

**"Lord, please hear our prayers and forgive our sins
and heal our land."**

Kill Zones

Murderous intent as he left home,
With nothing to lose-
Just hate to prove,
Schools have become kill zones.

Schools are no longer safe,
It is where the innocent die-
No more tears to cry,
Precious lives cannot be replaced.

We are numb to gun violence,
America should be ashamed-
Apathy is to blame,
Those in power are silent.

Politicians have no spine,
More guns than people-
Mass shootings is the sequel,
Our nation is in decline.

**"My sincerest condolences to all the families
across the country who have lost loved ones to
senseless acts of gun violence."**

American Greed And Plunder

So many went under,
Some barely afloat-
American greed and plunder,
Capsized the working-class boat.

Here comes another tide,
To make matters worse-
Many more have now died,
The vulnerable succumb first.

Nothing impedes like excess,
The rich want more-
The poor get less,
Few will make it to shore.

Who will throw a rope,
To those who still tread-
Hanging on to hope,
That better days are ahead.

"Oh how the poor are exploited."
-Coretta Scott King

Where Is The Love

We sit apart from each other,
We give our neighbors plenty of space-
We should come together as sisters and brothers,
Life is short and too precious to waste.

We do not care like we used too,
To be kind, some will not even try-
People will not speak sitting next to you,
Saying hi might get you the side eye.

Unforgiveness dwells in the core of us,
That is why we treat each other so bad-
But nowadays, who can you really trust,
Watching humanity decline is very sad.

Where did all the love go,
Love cast aside gives rise to hate-
What is inside is what you outwardly show,
Let us change course before it's too late.

**"When the love returns,
a sense of community will follow."**

The Heart and Soul

The soul is a bottomless well,
And has nine parts-
It is where hidden secrets dwell,
And cries out from a story to tell-
From all the pain inside the heart.

The heart has four chambers,
It is where our emotions reside-
It can be consumed with anger,
Rage run amuck can lead to danger-
And the reason why countless souls have died.

"Guard both with due diligence."

Candle Flames

On the rooftop I lay-
Beneath the moonlight,
Watching the candle flames sway.

They made me forget about my pain.
Then came the rain-
And washed my flames away.

**"If you can make it through the night there's a
brighter day."
-2Pac**

New Beginnings

Today is a good day,
For a new you to begin-
Ignore what critics say,
Refocus and start again.

The past is gone,
And will not return-
You must remain strong,
And apply what you learn.

Hold your head high,
Get rid of doubt-
Give it another try,
It will work out.

Failure is not the end,
It is only a test-
Your greatness lies within,
Give everything your best.

Fight the good fight,
Never settle for less-
Keep hope in sight,
Thy reward is success.

**"Trials and tribulations help to build character.
Don't give up, press on."**

Keep Going

Stay in your lane,
And play your part-
Push past your pain,
And never lose heart.

When up against the ropes,
Keep your vision in sight-
There is power in hope,
Swing with all your might.

You came here to win,
So do not give up-
If you fail, start again,
Success will not come by luck.

Whom God calls, He anoints,
Failure is the best teacher-
To reach your highest point,
You must dig much deeper.

**"Your success is predicated upon what you are
willing to endure to achieve it."**

Vengeance Is Mine
(God's Wrath On His Enemies)

When lightning strikes,
Like spiteful words-
Throughout the night,
Leaving foes unnerved.

The Lord is peeved,
With sinful man-
He now proceeds,
To smite the land.

He owns the cattle,
On a thousand hills-
The day of battle,
To enact His will.

Let the earth prepare,
For The Lord's return-
The wheat and tares,
Only one will burn.

**"It is mine to avenge, I will repay. In due time
their foot will slip; their day of disaster is near and
their doom rushes upon them."
Deuteronomy 32:35**

Why Am I Me

Why am I me,
And not someone else-
I seem to be,
At war with myself.

A severely flawed man,
Who truly means well-
Flesh rarely takes a stand,
And is prone to fail.

Will I ever be free,
From the condition I'm in-
Will I reach my destiny,
Or die in my sin.

Where did I go wrong,
Will I ever get right-
Today I press on,
For tomorrow's new fight.

**"I do not understand what I do. For what I want to
do, I do not do, but what I hate I do."
Romans 7:15**

True Friends

Who do you mean something too,
What if you have not been seen-
Who would be looking for you,
Would there be a search team.

If you were down on your luck,
And did not know what to do-
If you fell and got stuck,
Who would come to your rescue.

Who can you turn too,
Who can you depend on-
Who is playing chess with you,
And using you like a pawn.

Only call when they need help,
And always give you less-
They expect the best from everyone else,
But leave you drained and distressed.

Delete fake contacts,
Keep the ones who have your back-
Those with you through thick and thin,
They are your true friends.

**"Some people who you think are your friends, are
not friends at all. They are simply wolves in sheep
disguise."**

Empathy And Compassion

Scores of people are giving up,
Resist doing the same-
Pray for those who are out of touch,
And empathize with their pain.

We are living in desperate times,
Folks are on the edge and unstable-
Dealing with issues of the worst kind,
Unredeemable is how they're labeled.

How did they end up like that,
What happened along their journey-
Compassion may restore them back,
That could have been you or me.

Let us not ignore their plight,
Let us come to their rescue-
Poverty and mental health is a winnable fight,
Saving others is the least we can do.

"Give what you can. Do what you can. Say what
you can. Love while you can.
Don't hold back on yourself or others."

What If

What if you knew,
Things you never known.
What if you could do,
Things you were never shown.

What if you grew, and continued growing-
Every positive seed, keep on sowing.

"Sow and believe.
And nurture as needed."

The Struggle Is Real

It's a struggle to begin,
When consumed with the end-
Each thought is pending doom,
Troubled hearts, filled with gloom.

Then the mind debates,
Whether to let go-
Like excess weight,
But famished in the soul.

Then you self-analyze,
Fearing what you epitomize-
Suddenly you realize,
You have a see-through disguise.

What used to be dead,
Has now come alive-
Past things you've said,
Have now crystalized.

Void of self-love,
But in love with self-hate-
Seek relief from above,
Before it's too late.

But I duly confess,
The struggle is real-
Issues you don't address,
Come back with zeal.

"Every outside battle began within."

68

Confliction

Souls are unsatisfied,
Foundations are unstable-
A failure is how you're labeled,
And you are broken inside.

No will to carry on,
No trust in a guide-
When so many have lied,
Feeling like you don't belong.

When your skies are grey,
Who can you turn too,
To help get you through,
Because you are not okay.

There is no refuge,
No safe place of hope-
In vain you grope,
Strife is your deluge.

When you toss all night,
And wake up in pain,
Each day is the same-
Morning does not bring light.

No more strength to fight,
Confliction is to blame-
Tired of all the rain,
Never could get it right.

"God is close to the brokenhearted."
Psalms 34:18

Bleak

Overtime is never enough,
To make ends meet.
Low wages make life tough,
The outlook of some is bleak.

Unfit living conditions,
With nowhere else to go.
Each day brings new opposition,
Every stranger is a potential foe.

Not enough schooling to compete,
No reliable transportation.
Kids with no food to eat,
Lead to acts of desperation.

No cops on the beat,
Gangs have taken over.
Can't walk down the street,
Without looking over your shoulder.

**"Under paid and over worked,
and living in the ghetto."**

The Lord Knows

There is trouble down here,
Many hardships abound-
The path is not clear,
And hope cannot be found.

The Lord knows your pain,
And what you've been through-
He will take away the shame,
And your mind He will renew.

Move on from the past,
It is gone for a reason-
Trials were not meant to last,
Today is a new season.

Speak life to your situation,
There are better days ahead-
You have a glorious destination,
By His spirit be led.

"Stagnation is death."

Armageddon

Armageddon is brewing,
Fury from satans wrath-
The devil is now pursuing,
Those who reject his path.

He is released from his cage,
And has blood on his hands-
A beast full of rage,
Devouring all that he can.

Many will receive his mark,
And will go down in flames-
But saints are set apart,
Those called by God's name.

Christ will end his reign,
And will usher in peace-
Free from sin and pain,
Only love shall increase.

**"We are closer to this day than most people
think."**

The Dawn
(For My Best Friend, Sontae L. Massey)

It's the dawn of your season,
Time for you to be great-
You are reading this for a reason,
The best version of you awaits.

Days of stagnation are over,
Control is what you must take-
Wisdom to offer from being older,
A lasting impact you will make.

The door to your destiny,
You have keys to unlock-
Being a hero is your legacy,
To the lost who will knock.

Many lives will be saved,
From the work that you do-
And the path will be paved,
For generations after you.

"It's your season Tay, welcome to your harvest!"

Born 2 Fight
(When Your Enemies Underestimate You)
For Tiffany Hatchett

Life is not fair,
But I strive to do what is right-
Of pain, I've had my share,
But I was born 2 fight.

In The Lord I confide,
And walk toward the light-
Each step is in stride,
But I was born 2 fight.

Past your hate I see,
It fuels me to write-
I know who sustains me,
But I was born 2 fight.

You won't bring me down,
I sleep good at night-
Your karma will come around,
But I was born 2 fight.

**"What is yours is worth fighting for. Survive
everything. You will win in the end."**

Big Dreams

He dreamed of being on a movie screen,
But things are never what they seem-
Sound advice he would never take,
Until foolish pride sealed his fate.

He took off, but soon failed,
Not knowing grace was being withheld-
All his money he gambled and crapped,
Now wishing he had every roll back.

Life is short and cold,
But he was young, and could not be told-
What easily came, left the same,
And he has no one but himself to blame.

Now he is humbled and ready to listen,
And truly discover what he is missing-
He admits to not knowing it all,
And was blessed to recover from his fall.

**"Everything is not for you.
Only what God has for you is for you."**

Mental Therapy (The Power Of Poetry)

Released was long overdue,
My 1st book of poetry-
Miscellaneous Pieces was book 2,
FAME is book 3.

It got good, so I wrote more,
Did not know I had it in me-
Imagine is book 4,
Writing is mental therapy.

God gives talents to us,
To use for His glory-
He is worthy of our trust,
To continue His story.

Divinely inspired lyrics,
Can turn your life around-
Words that feed your spirit,
And lift you when you are down.

For ears ready to hear,
And eyes ready to see clear-
Your giants will disappear,
When faith has replaced fear.

"Poetry is life distilled."
-Gwendolyn Brooks

God's Example For Us

God is good,
And desires to help-
Like we should,
And do for self.

Permission to heal,
Begins with us-
Self-hate is real,
When taught to mistrust.

Let us strive to be,
Keepers of each other-
Replace I with we,
And uplift one another.

With a renewed mind,
Things can get better-
Now is the time,
To forgive and come together.

"The time is ripe to come together as a people."

The Turnaround (Jah's Grace And Mercy)

He ended up in a prison cell,
And dwelled without food or covers-
A sinner on his way to hell,
When the spirit of Jah hovered.

As he lay, he had a dream,
That he was given a scroll-
He was told to decode the unseen,
Everything that must soon unfold.

Things hidden from him came to light,
God's will for his life was revealed-
What is forbidden always seems right,
Nothing under the sun will be concealed.

He begged Jah to set him free,
And promised to never return-
Jah released him into his destiny,
He received what he was ready to learn.

Prepare your heart to hear his voice,
Anything broken can be made anew-
Those who hear must make a choice,
What is Jah saying to you.

**"The sacrifices of God are a broken spirit: a
broken and a contrite heart, O God, thou wilt not
despise.
Psalm 51:17**

Lost At Sea

In search of my destiny,
I set sail but got lost-
On a boat, but I was not free,
Unaware of the hidden cost.

Out on the open sea,
I was helpless and alone-
With no compass to guide me,
Back to the place I called home.

I did not know what to do,
I was lost, but could not turn around-
Life is a difficult maze to navigate through,
Searching, while hoping to be found.

Lord help me to change my course,
And deliver me from this storm-
Father, you are the life-giving source,
Please reveal my purpose for being born.

**"Not knowing your purpose in life is akin to being
lost and tossed at sea."**

Our Future Is In Our Hands

How did we end up here,
We have lost our way-
The reality of our plight is clear,
We must change course today.

Our children are lost,
And dying to be found-
Despair is a shared cost,
Enough pain to go around.

Elders have paved the way,
Was their labor in vain-
Division leads us further astray,
Then others profit from our pain.

Our condition is a fall from grace,
We need to be made whole-
For us to resume our rightful place,
Our race needs to get back on code.

**"Ancestral guidance is what we need to salvage
our communities."**

Scrutiny

This vicious level of scrutiny,
Designed to take me under-
But why come for me,
Is what I often wonder.

Even with all my flaws,
They still could not break me-
I am still standing tall,
Like I was destined to be.

I was raised to over-stand,
That God is in control-
I do not fear any man,
That is why I remain bold.

God has the last word,
Not those who hate me-
I will not be deterred,
I will reach my destiny.

"And Still I Rise."
-Dr. Maya Angelou

Self-Care And Oneness Of Humanity

No texts or calls please,
I need some me time-
To decompress and breathe,
And get spiritually aligned.

A cold world in despair,
Trauma and hate is passed down-
We need more people who care,
And positive words spread around.

We need to heal each other,
And let our collective light shine-
We need to live as sisters and brothers
And make better use of our time.

We need to come together,
And help each other win-
We should strive to do better,
And bring division to an end.

**"Let healing metastasize throughout the human
family (the body of our nation)."**

Stay Focused

Do not trip over petty shit,
Lose no sleep-
Be mindful of who you connect with,
Pray before you leap.

Know those who labor among you,
Are they there because they care-
Deceivers are adept at what they do,
Time is a costly thing to share.

Stay focused and don't lose hope,
What God has for you won't be denied-
Press on even when it's difficult to cope,
Your faith must be tested and tried.

You are almost at the finish line,
You have come too far to turn back-
Your reward will be worth the grind,
And you will never be in lack.

"There is no power on earth that can stop a determined soul."

The Pursuit

Life is a long race,
Never settle for second place-
Let no dream go to waste,
The reward is worth the chase.

"Pursue until you possess."

Be Yourself
(For My Dear, My Daughter Amaiya)

If you gotta be something,
Be yourself-
Angst is what you'll bring,
Trying to be someone else.

Change for betterment,
Not to fit in-
The time is far spent,
Make peace in your own skin.

Use your talents and gifts,
To uplift and inspire-
Satan's desire is to sift,
To keep you from going higher.

Separate from the crowd,
Pave your own way-
Let your actions speak loud,
Be true to you each day.

**"Stay in flight Dear.
Become all that you aspire to be."**

Our Steps (The Lord and I)

Lord, help me to let things go,
And put all my trust in you-
Teach me what I do not know,
Create in me something new.

Lord, please stay by my side,
Give me your words to say-
May we always be in stride,
Lead me every step of the way.

Lord, whatever is not good for me,
Do not let it enter my space-
May I walk only in destiny,
Strengthen me to finish the race.

Lord, I commit my life to you,
For your approval, I submit my plans-
Bless me in all that I do,
Help me to be a better man.

**"Dear God, help me to stay in stride with you.
Not my will, but thy will be done."**

Without You

I watch the gulls by the sea,
And mull how I wish life would be.

A trail of tears across the dock,
Marking time without a clock.

As I pace back and forth-
Life is truly too short.

No particular message to convey,
Other than I am missing you today.

**"Baby, I am completely lost without you.
Life doesn't mean the same to me anymore."**

Petty

Tit for tat,
I can be petty right back.
She did this, so I did that,
And we're both stuck in lack.

We both can't resist,
To sneak a diss.
What kind of relationship is this,
I thought we were passed the nonsense.

Mad for no good reason,
But we gotta get even.
Betrayal is a form of treason,
Now somebody is leaving.

Everyday it's the same song,
We just don't get along.
Where did we go wrong,
Our love used to be strong.

**"When being petty is the response, inventory
needs to be taken."**

Broken Hearted

Soft music,
Low sound-
Just me and my acoustic,
Watching the sun go down.

Wine and gentle breeze,
Help convey my thoughts-
My spirit tries to ease,
From feelings that I caught.

Pillow-soaked tears,
All night I toss-
Memories over the years,
Replay the love I lost.

What we shared was rare,
Can't believe we fell apart-
I am broken beyond repair,
From the anguish inside my heart.

"I love and miss you so much baby."

Epistles Read Of God

Each person is like a scroll,
That God has already read-
The scriptures tell us to behold,
The Son who was raised from the dead.

Your life is in His hands,
He knows His plans for you-
Those called by His name understand,
His will is what you must do.

When He knocks upon your heart,
Open up and invite Him in-
Favor upon you sets you apart,
To live a life free of sin.

Seek Him early in the day,
Cry out to Him at night-
He will give you what to say,
Serve Him with all thy might.

**"Today if you shall hear his voice, harden
not your hearts."
Psalm 95:8**

Swept Away
(The Day My Life Changed For The Worse)

The love of my life was swept away,
And a part of me died that day-
Oh my God is all I could say,
There is no peace when I lay.

This pain proves that hearts can break,
Love unconditionally before it's too late-
Not sure how much more I can take,
There is no peace when I wake.

She could no longer hold on,
The angry waves were just to strong-
Never imagined that she would be gone,
In my arms is where she belongs.

She was all I was living for,
Each day I miss her more and more-
Losing my baby hurts to my core,
Grief stricken as I wall along the shore.

"Some losses you don't recover from."

Life Is.......

Life is like a vapor.
We are easily erased words-
On a thin piece of paper.

Life is like a nightmare.
With no real meaning-
Among people who don't care.

Life is like a prison without bars.
The blackest, moonless sky-
Without any stars.

Life is like a bad song.
That plays in your head-
And never moves on.

Life is like a tropical storm.
Destroying everything in its path-
Leaving you battered and scorned.

Life is like a bad joke.
That nobody gets-
Like the horse chasing a carrot on a rope.

Life is like a dirty mirror.
That is full of cracks-
And your self-image looks inferior.

Life is like a broken clock.
That couldn't be fixed-
After it was dropped.

Life is like a roadblock.
When you are pressed for time-
After opportunity knocked.

Life is like an unfair game.
That each generation plays-
But the outcome remains the same.

Life is like the prodigal son.
Who never returns-
Like a kingdom that never comes.

"The perils in life are never ending."

Remember
(When You Are Feeling Some Type Of Way)

Remember how far you have come,
And what you overcame to get here-
Remember what you have been delivered from,
And despite the odds, how you persevered.

Remember that you are enough,
Take a deep breath, and slowly exhale-
Remember all the times you got back up,
And not the number of times you fell.

For healing, watch the sunset,
Or publish your thoughts in a book-
Do not give power to regrets,
And backwards, never look.

To reduce stress, meditate,
And choose to forgive-
For the mind to be in a better state,
It must find a reason to live.

**"One must have accomplishments in order to
have something to reflect upon.
Rebounding from low moments will show what
you are made of
and will help keep high moments in perspective."**

The Purpose Of Being (For Undra Ware)

The universe is alive,
An array of planets- strategically aligned.
Living things were created to thrive-
Purposely designed- by the hand of the divine.

Misinformation plagues the nation,
Voices from hell- seek to drown out truth.
Negative seeds are sown without hesitation-
To poison the minds- of our impressionable youth.

Division is leading to a cosmic collision,
Nothing alive- will survive the collide.
Conditions for life took pinpoint precision-
Unity alone- is the only way to thrive.

The purpose of being is striving to be,
The best version- of your authentic self.
To fulfill God's will and reach your destiny-
Love for one another- the only true wealth.

**"Thank you brother for sharing your gift of poetry.
You are inspiring the world with your talents
(your purpose for being).
Continued blessings to you and yours."**

The Kingship Of The Black Man
(Dedicated To Chadwick Boseman, R.I.P. King)

11/29/76  **8/28/2020**

The Black man is legendary-
The original King.
Subduer of land and sea-
By his side is his Queen.

Gives everything his all-
Never holds back.
With his God he stands tall-
Nothing does he lack.

A leader in his home-
He guides and protects.
Always mindful of his tone-
And gets treated with respect.

Has a confident stride-
Full of compassion as well.
In service to others, he abides-
His legacy, generations will tell.

"Our King Forever."

Memories

Memories are made daily-
And guide what we do.
Thoughts only we can see,
Recording what we've been through.

Some memories help us grow-
Others keep us in lack.
Memories can be a friend or foe,
Seeds planted can't be taken back.

Bad memories get bold-
And breed fear and doubt.
Some memories never get told,
Those not worth talking about.

Memories of love we appreciate-
Are worth their weight in gold.
Whatever is sown will replicate,
Special moments never grow old.

"Cherished memories are priceless."

Mysteries Of The Universe
(Heavenly Wonders)

What is out there,
Beyond what we see.
Stars above are extraordinaire,
And help guide our destiny.

What is out there,
They don't tell us that.
So we explore elsewhere,
Some won't make it back.

What is out there,
What are they trying to hide.
Secrets no one wants to share,
Although what we need is inside.

What is out there,
No one knows for sure.
Soon, everything will be laid bare,
Exposing what is not pure.

What is out there,
Is it possible to know.
I marvel, and can't help but stare,
Tonight, another star-studded show.

"I wonder."

The Relay

Watching my dad die,
Was a new low-
Plenty of tears to cry,
All have a time to go.

Our days are numbered,
Earth is our temporal home-
What is beyond, I often wonder,
Every seed must be sown.

Each death is a relay,
The torch must be passed-
Life is given, then taken away,
Nothing seen will last.

Life is but a mist,
We are born to decay-
Memories are made to reminisce,
Take nothing for granted today.

"Rest easy dad."
Frederick Edward Horton Sr.
Sunrise: January 10, 1950,
Sunset: June 11, 2022

Trauma

I returned and took a look,
But didn't remember seeing this-
My life is an open book,
But it's painful to reminisce.

I experienced traumatic things,
And wished I was dead-
Trauma is what this life brings,
Childhood secrets left unsaid.

I fought this battle alone,
Leary of who to trust-
Family and fake friends cast stones,
And kick up the most dust.

Life is an uphill journey,
Haunting grief most of the time-
If so inclined, remember me,
Inner peace I could never find.

"Behind every mask, there is hidden trauma."

Under The Sun

We are born to see the sun,
Although there is nothing new under it-
Don't die with your works undone,
Take a break, but don't quit.

Daily we are becoming,
Trust the process-
Trials are not for succumbing,
Tests help you appreciate success.

Your effort and faith matters,
Stay encouraged along the way-
It seems like a never-ending ladder,
Keep climbing and ignore what critics say.

Who knows what's on the other side,
Just get it right while you're here-
No shame, means there is nothing to hide,
After death, means there is nothing to fear.

**"Like Jesus, work the works of Him that sent you.
Work while it's day, when night cometh, no one
can work. Always be a light, especially on dark
days."**

His Son Again

Lord, help me to find my way,
And bless me to stay the course-
Now I am willing to obey,
For my shortcomings, I have remorse.

Please forgive me for going astray,
I endeavor to do things right-
Thank you Lord for another day,
And for keeping me through the night.

I want to be Your son again,
And live by your decrees and commands-
On your grace my life depends,
On your promises I will stand.

Thank you Lord for my new beginning,
Being received has given me renewed life-
Your love and forgiveness has no ending,
Redeemed from the finished work of Jesus Christ.

**"I will set out and go back to my father and say to him:
Father, I have sinned against Heaven and against you."
Luke 15:18**

Vibrations

What vibe do you bring,
What will others get-
Is it befitting a King or Queen,
Is it something to respect.

Is your energy high or low,
Does it repel or attract-
Do blessings follow wherever you go,
When you leave, do others want you back.

Do people look forward to seeing you,
Are they happy when you come around-
Does your presence add any value,
Or does your aura bring people down.

Treat others how you want to be treated,
Smile and look people in the eye-
Healing and unconditional love is what is needed,
Exchange kind words before saying goodbye.

**"I aspire to vibrate higher. Therefore, I only want
positive and healing vibes around me."**

Peaceful Sleep In Restless Times

Let the peaceful sleep,
Let the restless stay up-
Let the peaceful reach their peak,
Let the restless drink from a bitter cup.

"There is no rest unto the wicked."
Isaiah 48:22

Prayed Up
(Take Nothing For Granted)

Pray before you lay,
That you make it through the night-
Give thanks when you see another day,
Another chance to get it right.

Greet the sun with a smile,
Like the sun, you rise to shine-
Have the gratitude of a little child,
As you embark upon today's grind.

While at work, give it your best,
What you have, others are praying for-
Embrace small beginnings and trust the process,
And The Lord will bless you with more.

Many left home, but not all returned,
So take nothing for granted-
God's best, may you wisely discern,
And may you arrive safely wherever you're planted.

"An attitude of gratitude is everything."

10 Affirmations

Affirmation-1
Destiny is ahead of you,
Your gift will make room-
To your calling stay true,
Stay humble as you bloom.

Affirmation-2
You are the worlds flame-
Stay lit at all times.

Affirmation-3
What you say is what you'll have-
Don't speak when you are mad.

Affirmation-4
Never quit.

Affirmation-5
You are the promised seed,
God planted you for a reason-
He will water and meet every need,
This is your winning season.

Affirmation-6
Your future is bright,
Keep your vision in sight.
When the road gets rough, persist-
The reward is worth the risk.

Affirmation-7
Don't stray from the path,
Keep walking towards the light-
What's done for God will last,
You're destined for greater heights.

Affirmation-8
You must start to get there,
You must persevere to achieve-
Life wasn't promised to be fair,
Success comes those who believe.

Affirmation-9
Do more and say less,
Actions are your speech-
Each day give your best,
And God will extend your reach.

Affirmation-10
What others need, you got,
You're their source of inspiration-
Without you, they'll remain in the same spot,
Your light helps them see their destination.

"Let us affirm ourselves and one another daily."

Next Level Destiny

Put the world on mute,
Give negative people the boot.
Then stretch out in an open field,
And ponder what's next to build.

Let your imagination run free,
And speak your next level destiny.
To be more than what you are,
A light brighter than any star.

What's inside must come to fruition,
Time alone is the only thing missing.
Gifts were given for a reason,
And now it's winning your season.

It's okay if others don't understand,
Believe in yourself and formulate a plan.
Many are called but the chosen are few,
Stay encouraged and let nothing derail you.

"Your vision is for your eyes only."

Life, The Moving Screen

Life is a moving screen,
A repetitive story with familiar scenes.
We were cast as unwitting actors,
And judged accordingly in the hereafter.

"What we see has been seen before."

Fleeting Time

Yesterday won't come back-
Today won't last forever.
Death is a matter of fact-
Love is the highest endeavor.

"There is a limited time to express love."

The Wisdom Of Nature And The Hourglass We're Up Against

Water sustains life and has memory,
Trees breathe and know their offspring-
Honeybees add value to our economy,
Hoping for a mate, the morning birds sing.

Life is short and we need each other,
Everyone has something to offer-
I would not be here without my brother,
I pray that hardened hearts get softer.

We are here today, but a memory tomorrow,
Make amends while you can-
The time we have down here is borrowed,
The hourglass is almost out of sand.

Love is an action word,
And is measured by sacrifice-
Without compassion and a willingness to serve,
Nature and humanity will pay the price.

"Nature nourishes. And we are charged to do the same for ourselves and each other."

Everyday Death

Today was someone's last day,
Loved ones will gather to mourn and pray.

Hearts will be filled with pain and sorrow-
It will be the same tomorrow.

"Death is no respecter of persons."

Last Words

A series of moments,
That's what life is-
Obstacles are akin to opponents,
And make life hard to live.

You believe you have time when you're young,
But it doesn't always work that way-
Many took unhealthy risks and succumbed,
And didn't get to see another day.

Karma is real,
Every temptation is a test-
Forgive in order to heal,
Strive for excellence and never settle for less.

Keep a watch on your wrist,
Value and enjoy the time you have-
Never say goodbye without a kiss,
Moments captured helps getting through days that
are bad.

**"My son, hear the instruction of your father, and
do not forsake the law of your mother.
For they will be a graceful ornament on your head
and a chain of honor around your neck."
Proverbs 1:8**

The Downside Of Social Media

Social media is used to incite,
Take heed to what you read-
Trolls live to pick a fight,
Time wasted is where it leads.

Do not feed into all the hype,
Their agenda is to make money-
My truth lies within what I write,
Character assassination has never been funny.

Some things people don't rebound from,
What you easily ignore, affects others differently-
Getting caught up could happen to anyone,
Petty beefs often lead to tragedy.

Hearts and likes are tied to self-esteem,
We were better connected before Facebook-
It doesn't exist if it's not posted and seen,
Social media has the whole world hooked.

"Use responsibly."

Diminished

He wrote from the heart,
And spoke from the same-
In poetic circles he made his mark,
And he relished in the fame.

A rags to riches story,
He was loved everywhere he went-
But he never gave God the glory,
Money he did not have was already spent.

He did not stay true to who he was,
He thought it was all about him-
His devout fans took away their love,
The light he once had is now dim.

He spends his days and nights sulking,
Too ashamed to make a comeback-
Naïve to the traps that being famous brings,
He needed more than talent to stay on track.

**"But when his heart became arrogant and
hardened with pride, he was deposed from his
royal throne and stripped of his glory."
Daniel 5:20**

For Your Consideration

Overthinkers, overthink to protect,
They weigh every possible scenario-
Whatever you give, you always get,
So plant positive seeds wherever you go.

Loss happens, but don't lose self-respect,
Keep your dignity and self-esteem high-
People with negative vibes, be quick to disconnect,
Live your truth and not their lie.

Pay no mind to critics on the sideline,
Those who do the least say the most-
Haters who doubted you will be left behind,
But you will have a success story to post.

People project on you what they cannot do,
Miserable people have their own crowd-
Work hard, stay focused and see it through,
You will make the only person that matters proud.

**"What you believe about yourself matters the
most. Don't overthink and under act."**

Life's Pressure

Life was 2 much 2 handle,
Everyone expected so much-
The mind sometimes can become scrambled,
And you feel out of touch.

"What else do they want from me,
I gave them everything I had-
Now I just want to be free,
Outward smile, but inwardly sad."

"The pressures and stresses of life are very real.
Anyone can succumb in moments of despair and
feelings of hopelessness."
The National Suicide Prevention Lifeline: 800-273-
8255, or dial, 988.
Or visit: SpeakingOfSuicide.com.

Hurting People Hurt Others And Sometimes Kill

Where are you,
And how did you get there-
Do you even have a clue,
Or do you even care.

Look at what you've become,
Another number locked away-
Internal issues you can't outrun,
This kind goes away when you fast and pray.

Your actions took innocent lives,
Loved ones hearts you've ripped apart-
Without grace you will meet your demise,
A painful death in the dark.

Some people are sick and lost,
Damaged souls need to be healed-
From their trauma, others pay the cost,
Hurting people hurt others and sometimes kill.

"How unfortunate it is when innocent people have to bear the brunt of other people's trauma. Life is so unfair!"

What People Need

People need love, hope, and inspiration to carry on-
No one is always strong.

**"Everyone gets weary at times. And everyone is
going through something, real or imagined.
Be compassionate and lend a helping hand or a
listening ear."**

Maturity
(Letting Go Of The Past)

I sat and watched the waves,
To unwind and clear my mind-
Unresolved trauma keeps you enslaved,
And makes happiness hard to find.

To be released is a feast,
For many years I failed to enjoy-
Trapped inside the belly of the beast,
From issues as a little boy.

Much I missed from not letting go,
On the past I held a tight grip-
Forgiving is the only way to grow,
Not forgiving is a sinking ship.

I could not fly carrying dead weight,
Letting go is a sign of maturity-
The life I want I must create,
It feels good to finally be free.

**"If it doesn't serve you, let it go. Letting go is
proof that you're ready to grow."**

Destiny Leader Rose
(The Determined, Focused And Unstoppable Rose)
For Lyrical 7

A leader rose grew from concrete,
In spite of the oppressors feet.
This rose was destined to grow,
Her worth, she was determined to show.

Many envied her grace and splendor,
Firm stem, but her pedals were tender.
Each day she reached for the sun,
Knowing that she was second to none.

Other flowers wilted from her presence,
They did not possess her divine essence.
This rose refused to be victimized,
Instead she chose to self-actualize.

She bloomed into her destiny,
Becoming all she desired to be.
A message to anyone who will listen,
You can grow too despite opposition.

"No matter the circumstance, it's your duty and responsibility to grow."

Freedom Or Defeat
(Choose Wisely)

Wanna be free?
Love unconditionally and practice humility.

Wanna live in defeat?
Feed your greed and practice deceit.

"The formula."

You Got This

Life is tough, but so are you-
Don't give up, adjust your view.

**"See yourself as an overcomer
and set your sights higher."**

Resilience

It takes heart to start,
Power within to begin–
If you fall, don't fall apart,
Quitting is the only sin.

"Prove it to yourself. Jump in and win."

Decisions Decisions

Run or fight,
Divide or unite-
Sleep or rise,
Be seen or hide.

Stay or leave,
Doubt or believe-
Work or play,
Rebel or obey.

Live or die,
Give up or try-
Tell the truth or lie,
Be sober or high.

Spend or save,
Eat or crave-
Stop or go,
Regress or grow.

Choices are your voice, so be decisive in your decision making.

"A double minded man is unstable is all his ways."
James 1:8

Yesterday
(The Day That Wouldn't Go Away)

Is today a new day,
Or is it just hungover-
Still drunk from yesterday,
And can't get sober.

Is today a continuation,
Of yesterday's indignation-
Everything happens for a reason,
Yesterday is still getting even.

Today is like Déjà Vu,
Yesterday will not leave me alone-
Today has been hard to get through,
In the past is where yesterday belongs.

I hope tomorrow is a better day,
Yesterday and today was very tough-
Did I attract what came my way,
Tomorrow cannot come soon enough.

**"Let hope for a better tomorrow be your
inspiration for today."**

Health Conscious

Energy comes from Vitamin D,
Arise and get you some sun-
Ride your bike, walk, or run,
Alone, or with company.

Yoga and Tai chi,
Are good for the mind-
Helps you get spiritually aligned,
Drink elderberry and chamomile tea.

Open up your third eye,
Your mind is a prism-
Reset your circadian rhythm,
Give sea moss a try.

It's about being healthy,
Exercise and good nutrition-
Are keys to your body's ignition,
Results take consistency.

"Good health is the new wealth."

Riptide
(Memories Of Pain)

Waves of blame,
I ride in my mind.
Trauma and scars remain,
Healing is blind.

"I wish healing had eyes and would find me."

My Understanding Of Life

What is loved, will be kissed,
What is lost, will be missed-
What is free, will be bound,
What is up, will come down.

What is heavy, will be light,
What is wrong, will be right-
What is high, will be low,
What is fast, will be slow.

What is stable, will be crumbled,
What is proud, will be humbled-
What is good, will be bad,
What is happy, will be sad.

What is clean, will be dirty,
What is fragile, will be sturdy-
What is soft, will be hard,
What is healed, will be scarred.

"Life is an evolving, complex circle."

Judgers Among Us (Stone Casters)

Who really knows you,
Better than yourself-
Strangers have a limited view,
But are quick to judge someone else.

They lurk in the comments section,
Cast stones, then hide their hand-
Racist trolls are masters of projection,
Hate is what they want to expand.

They are not concerned with truth,
They only sow seeds of division-
Quick to condemn without proof,
That's how gossipers make their living.

But soon the tables will turn,
Hidden foes will be exposed-
Some fools will never learn,
Receipts on them will be a trove.

**"There are six things The Lord hates, seven that are
detestable to him. Haughty eyes, a lying tongue, hands
that shed innocent blood, a heart that devises wicked
schemes, feet that are quick to rush into evil, a false
witness who pours out lies and a person who stirs up
conflict in the community."**
Proverbs 6: 16-19

Where Unhappiness Lives

Where unhappiness lives,
Something has to give-
The concealed place of pain,
Where unearthed trauma remains.

Deep inside the soul,
Memories never grow old-
Too ashamed to share,
And issues never go anywhere.

Release to God and be healed,
No one else has to know-
Everything does not need revealed,
True repentance is how you grow.

Today is the day to say enough,
It starts with a made-up mind-
No more beating yourself up,
You have wasted enough money and time.

"Be healed and be blessed in Jesus name."

Start The Healing Process (Forgive Yourself And Others) And Be Blessed

Let peace reign inside your heart,
Forgive yourself and others-
If you fall, don't fall apart,
Give yourself permission to recover.

You can't win, if you don't start,
Begin, and see it to the end-
On the world, place your mark,
And be your own best friend.

You owe yourself more than this,
Let this be your last loss-
Believe and receive your every wish,
God's grace will cover the cost.

It is time for the real you,
The person you were destined to be-
To prove dreams do come true,
As a witness for the world to see.

**"You deserve to be the best version of yourself.
Know that good things are in store for you.
Believe in yourself, trust God, and never give up."**

Pretenders
(Fake Friends)

Pretenders will turn on you,
And you won't see it coming-
Secretly hate is what they do,
Betrayal of fake friends is stunning.

These type I won't miss,
Laughing when things go wrong-
The simple truth is this,
They were enemies all along.

Wishing your success was theirs,
Jealous of everything you do-
They front and put on airs,
True friends are few.

I got me a new crowd,
It was time for the next level-
Now only my actions speak loud,
Never again will I settle.

"Things aren't always what they seem."

Keep It Real

Secrets always tell and show,
So keep it real with your issues-
You need time away to grow,
Even if people miss you.

Seek refuge in a private place,
Let God speak to your soul-
Trust in His amazing grace,
For things beyond your control.

Like minded friends are essential,
Those who believe in you-
Pushing you to reach your potential,
Master what you set out to do.

Stop blowing in the wind,
For your life, God has a plan-
On your story someone will depend,
It is time to possess the land.

"Everyone won't understand your journey or your assignment, and that's ok. Stay true to you and make it happen."

T.I.M.E
(Today It Might End)

Are you a wise manager of your time,
Are you doing what you're supposed to do-
You can't go back and press rewind,
Your time is God's gift to you.

**"Days are not promised, they're numbered.
Make your time count."**

HA**I**KU

**M
A
G
I
N
E**
s**E**ction

The Weather Inside

The weather inside,
Is where your focus should be-
It matters the most.

Stunted

As a kid he died.
He did not mature inside-
Yet, he's still alive.

The Truth

Don't ignore the truth.
It could save your life one day-
Heed the warning signs.

Trust The Process

It takes time to grow.
Nothing meant to last, comes fast-
Greatness takes patience.

Bliss

The sea covers me.
On land, there's no privacy-
Beneath I swim free.

The Balcony

My bed is out there.
Overlooking the ocean-
I rise with the sun.

Derailed

A soldier no more.
Derailed by the perfect storms-
Cost me my career.

Unbothered

Nothing that you say,
Makes me feel a certain way-
So don't waste your time.

Sacred Locs

Locs are spiritual.
Spiral strands are in demand-
Twist your hair with care.

Bottom Dwellers

Stuck at the bottom.
Excuses is all they know-
No vision to grow.

Trauma

Nightmares when she sleeps.
Trauma has sullied her dreams-
She lives in defeat.

Mother Earth

To hear her heartbeat,
I put my ear to the ground-
And was comforted.

Cocoon

Change was taking place.
Flight is a personal choice-
She found her own voice.

The Past

My dirty laundry,
Is not open for debate-
You have a pile too.

My Word

My word is my bond.
People are counting on me,
I won't let them down.

Self-Care

Take care of yourself.
You have a lot to live for-
Don't ever give up.

Love

Love is what we need.
Without love, we are nothing-
Start loving yourself.

Clean Hands

No one has clean hands.
Just care enough to wash them,
We all have a past.

Book Sales

Imagine this book,
Selling a million copies-
That would be so nice.

Weight Loss

I need to lose weight.
Then I need to keep it off-
Maintaining is key.

Poetry

Poetry is life.
Life started with a concept,
Then it became real.

Money

I need more money.
Being broke don't work for me-
I'm better than this.

Focused

My mind is made up.
I am never going back-
Too much to live for.

Purposeful Living

What is your calling?
What did you come here to do-
Someone needs your gift.

Help Out

Help someone in need.
You may need that same help soon-
That's why you don't judge.

Reach Out

We know what to do,
Or say to make someone's day-
Don't hold back, reach out.

Talk Is Cheap

If talk wasn't cheap,
The poor would not have a voice-
They would only write.

Longevity

Don't be negative.
Hang with positive people-
You will live longer.

Remembering Me

At my funeral,
Speak about the good I did-
And I'll rest in peace.

Bonus Haiku

Each One Teach One

No one knows it all,
We learn something new each day-
Truth is infinite.

Bonus Poem

Servanthood
(The Love That Keeps Giving And Going)
For Angela Thomas Smith, Queen of
Collaborations

You have had many sleepless nights,
And your fair share of despair-
Forsaken by people you thought would care,
Yet, your smile remains bright.

In a world so unfair and cold,
You are a beacon for the downtrodden-
Those who society has forgotten,
Your unflinching stand for justice is bold.

Your energy is envied and unmatched,
Unconditional love reigns in your heart-
Being fearless sets you apart,
Compassion for others, keep people attached.

Your heavenly crown awaits you,
You have served God's people well-
Your legacy of love others will tell,
To the call of servanthood, you remained true.

**"For America to reach its glory, Black Women will lead
the way, imagine that."
~Stay Strong Queens~**

Made in the USA
Monee, IL
02 September 2023

41998016R00079